WAR VOICES

Also by Tony Curtis

Poetry

Taken for Pearls
The Last Candles

Anthologies

The Poetry of Pembrokeshire
The Poetry of Snowdonia
Love from Wales (with Siân James)

Critical

Dannie Abse
How to Study Modern Poetry
The Art of Seamus Heaney (ed)
How Poets Work (ed)
Wales: The Imagined Nation (ed)

WAR VOICES

TONY CURTIS

seren

seren
is the book imprint of
Poetry Wales Press Ltd
Wyndham Street, Bridgend, Mid Glamorgan
Wales

© Tony Curtis, 1995

A Cataloguing in Publication record for this title is available
from the British Library CIP Data Office

ISBN 1-85411-141-8

All rights reserved. No part of this publication my be reproduced,
stored in a retrieval system, or transmitted in any way or by any means,
electronic, mechanical, photocopying, recording or otherwise,
without the prior permission of the publisher.

The publisher acknowledges the financial support of the
Arts Council of Wales

Cover Illustration:
Stanley Spencer: 'Unveiling the Cookham War Memorial
Private Collection
Transparency courtesy of the Royal Academy

Printed in Palatino
by WBC Book Manufacturers Ltd

For all my families:
Barlow, Barrah, Curtis and Williams

CONTENTS

Through fields of white crosses

9   From the City that Shone
11 William Orpen and Yvonne Aubicq at the Rue Dannon
13 The Front
14 The Last Candles
16 The Death of Richard Beattie-Seaman in the Belgian Grand Prix
18 Incident on a Hospital Train from Calcutta
19 The Last Soldier
20 The World
21 From the Hills, the Town

The watchers

25 Brady's Glass
26 The Captain's Diary
29 Home Front
30 Poles
31 Dedicating the House of Art
33 Villanelle for a Photographer
34 Crane Flies
36 At Sligo, 1976
38 The Watchers

The rattle of bullets in the trees

41 Lessons
42 Soup
43 The Visit to Terezin
44 Trials
46 The Portrait of Hans Theo Richter and his Wife Gisela, Dresden, 1933

48   Friedhof
50   Boxes
52   Kalavryta
53   The Bowl and Spoon

This drawing of lines from memory

57   Sporting Pigs Frieze
58   Couples from the Fifties
60   Pictures in a School Hall
61   The Grammar
63   My Great Uncle Charlie
66   Pine Baron
67   Lines at Barry
69   At Ochrid Lake
70   Belgium: Coffee
71   Reg Webb
72   Guard Duty
74   Veteran: South Dakota
75   Manouvres on Kinder Scout
77   Window Seat to Chicago
78   In McDonough County
79   Land Army Photographs

Through fields of white crosses

From the City that Shone

The thing we dreamt of most was a bath:
so we crossed the wire and made for Gonnelieu
where, it was said, a tin bath lay abandoned
near the well of the convent school.
We kept to ruined shadows down the street,
towels and soap in our haversacks.

John had a canvas bucket and filled it from the well.
The bath held firm, the water cold and sweet.
I lorded it there in the weedy garden
amidst the ransacked books strewn all about,
broken glass wicked in the sun,
then towelled dry while
John tipped the water across the grass.

I drew fresh water for him and passed the soap.
'I always sing,' he said.
'Too risky.'
But he splashed and hummed
— *And who shall kiss her ruby lips*
When I am far away? —

I sat on the path, my hair drying,
my head thrown back to the clearing sky
where a Taube stuttered through clouds from the West.
In those moments before the guns started up
it seemed that summer was held in place.

John rose from the water
'Like a god,' he said,
his arms outstretched, then lobbed the soap
grenade-like at my head.
It squirted past me, diving in the slips.
We dressed
— each stuck a dog-rose in his tunic —
and turned back to our trenches.

Pressed into the shadows, I thought:
What does all this mean?
Two young soldiers, for a moment
Sunday-school clean in all this mess.
The Taube crossed overhead, coughing smoke,
and made desperate way to his own lines.

William Orpen & Yvonne Aubicq in the Rue Dannon

This morning he wakes early —
sun and the sounds of carts in the streets
coming through the roughly-drawn curtains,
a fine March light over the city.
She has lain an arm across his shoulder.
In sleep her beauty is muted, held somewhere
ringing like the glint of a far-off bell.
He has seen them in ruins, the churches,
the chateaux, the empty, crumbling town squares.
He has coloured them green against brown,
yellow against dirt, the torn bodies,
the green limbs under shell-hole water.
He dreamt of lobsters moving behind glass
in the restaurant at the Savoy.
Yvonne stirs under his breath,
her sleeping face turns halfway to his.
The head is perfect under night-tousled hair,
her eyelids shimmer like butterflies' wings.
There is painting and life and death.
The mayor's beautiful daughter lies in his bed.
He is having a good war.

Last August baked the mud of the Somme
into a pure, dazzling white. And there
were daisies, blood-red poppies
and a blue flower, for miles it seemed,
great masses of blue that were,
close-to, particular delicacies.
The sky a pure, dark blue and the whole air
for thirty feet up or more quivered
with white butterflies. I brushed them — I was gentle — from
my uniform as I returned to the car.
We drove on through fields of white crosses,
the butterflies slamming against my driver's glass,
as if those crosses lurched out of the unsettled earth.

At Thiepval I began to paint a trench.
It held the remnants of two soldiers
— one German, one of ours..

*I could not hold the sight for too long at a time
so gave myself rest against the torn trunk of a tree.
Three sessions, an hour passed, and then
a loose shell came over and burst.*

*I was blown backwards head over arse.
My heavy portrait easel took the force
— a skull smashed up through the canvas —
and the whole scene was blown to hell.*

He slips away from her embrace
and she murmurs in sleep.
Tomorrow or the next day it will be complete —
the light on that slope of her left shoulder,
more work on the hair perhaps. He'll
watch her comb it as he loads his palette.
He has caught her classically
holding herself back from one's gaze,
arms crossed over her breasts
pulling her robe to her right shoulder.
That teasing look will devastate.

He rises, wraps the robe about himself
and crosses to the window to light a cigarette.
From the balcony he blows smoke over Paris.

*At the end of the Rue Dannon is a square.
This is where they will march her — yes
I'll say she is a spy — call her Frida Neiter —
a spy for the Boche that the French will shoot.
She does not scream or struggle,
but walks upright, across the road
to the wall.
As the soldiers raise their rifles and
the officer his sword, she lets
slip her fur coat to the ground.
Naked she stands to face them,
her arms held out from her sides.*

It seems a lifetime before they fire.

The Front

He took a bullet
and fell.
I went down to him
ducked under their fire.

I have you
It's alright
I said.

Pulling his arms around my neck
I carried him back
to the safety of our line.
His face was wet against my neck.

They did not let up
the whole way.

Taking bullets all the while
he died against me
and I wore him
like a pelt
my shield
my brother
my other skin.

The Last Candles

The final stage of our journey over
we reached Odessa. So glorious
a scene I think my eyes had never taken in —
the harbour bristling with ships of all the allied nations.
We were received at the consulate by a young man,
fresh and clean in a crisp English suit.
Courteous and gentlemanly. I had not seen
such a man for four years.

In the hotel that night my dreams were of uniforms
and wounds, but one wound served for many —
thus, a severed arm at Biyech, the lacerated
stomach of a boy in Khutanova, the bloody head
of a captured Turk in Noscov — and then swabs
fell like the first snows of Winter,
the land chill and beyond pain
under its bandages.

For breakfast we were offered good bread and an egg.
The smell of coffee made me dizzy.

At nine we leave for the harbour. The streets
packed with aimless crowds, though everything
makes way for the *Bolsheviki* in their lorries.
At the harbour gates a man of no apparent rank
holds our papers for an hour.
He has a rifle and a long knife hangs
from his belt. A red band has been clumsily
sewn to the sleeve of his coat.

Some of the Norwegian crew speak English.
My cabin proves small, but warm.
After years under canvas, sheltering in ruins,
nursing beneath shattered roofs,
I am glad to call it home.
Though the place is strange and metallic
after stone and wood and earth.
Doctor Rakhil calls to take me on deck
for our departure.

            Ten years of living in this great land
have brought me to love it.
Though three of those years have been spent in war,
and then this anarchy, this revolution.

I see Odessa under red flags
as we cast off and the engines churn.
I feel everything moving away from me
as if Russia were a carpet being rolled to the sky.
At the harbour mouth Doctor Rakhil
gently turns me from the rail,
but is not quite quick enough.

That night, the sea pressing around me,
I dream of three things —
a day in Moscow, when Nadya and I
were close enough to reach out and touch
the Tsar, and an old peasant
who had crawled through the crowd, between
the legs of the guards, clutching
his ragged petition,
still calling out as their boots struck him.
Nicholas II, Tsar of all the Russias, flickered
his eyes, but his step was the unfaltering
step of a god.
                My first dead man
in the training ward. Grey and small in the candlelight,
his mouth like a closed purse and what seemed
to be butterflies on his face. Two sugarlumps
to weigh down his eye-lids.

            And at last, this leaving
Odessa. How in the shadows I saw them —
officers from the front fleeing the chaos of desertion
and caught by the Reds at the port.
They bound their feet to heavy stones
and planted them in the harbour. Swaying, grey shapes
I glimpsed from the rail, as if bowing to me.
The last candles of my Russia
guttering and going out under the black sea.

The Death of Richard Beattie-Seaman in the Belgian Grand Prix, 1939

Trapped in the wreckage by his broken arm
he watched the flames flower from the front end.
So much pain — Holy Jesus, let them get to me —
so much pain he heard his screams like music
when he closed his eyes — the school organ at Rugby,
Matins with light slanting down
hot and heady from the summer's high windows.
Pain — his trousers welded by flame to his legs.
His left hand tore off the clouded goggles —
rain falling like light into the heavy trees,
the track polished like a blade.
They would get to him, they were all coming
all running across the grass, he knew.

The fumes of a tuned Mercedes smelt like
boot polish and tear gas — coughing, his screams rising
high out of the cockpit — high
away back to '38 Die Nurburgring.
He flew in with Clara
banking and turning the Wessex through a slow circle
over the scene — sunlight flashing off the line of cars,
people waving, hoardings and loudspeakers, swastikas
and the flags of nations lifted in the wind he stirred.
She held his arm tightly, her eyes were closed.
He felt strong like the stretched wing of a bird,
the course mapped out below him.
That day Lang and Von Brauchitsch and Caracciola
all dropped out and he did it — won
in the fourth Mercedes before a crowd of half a million
— the champagne cup, the wreath around his neck,
An Englishman the toast of Germany
The camera caught him giving a Hitlergruss.

Waving arms, shouts and faces, a mosaic
laid up to this moment — La Source— tight — the hairpin
in the trees — tight — La Source — keeping up the pace
Belgium — La Source hairpin too tight.

With the fire dying, the pain dying,
the voices blurred beneath the cool licks of rain.
To be laid under the cool sheets of rain.
A quiet with, just perceptible, engines roaring
as at the start of a great race.

Incident on a hospital train from Calcutta, 1944

At a water-stop three hours out
the dry wail of brakes ground us down
from constant jolting pain to an oven
heat that filled with moans and shouts
from wards the length of six carriages.

We had pulled slowly up towards the summer
hills for coolness. They were hours distant,
hazy and vague. I opened the grimy
window to a rush of heat
and, wrapped in sacking, a baby

held up like some cooked offering from its mother —
Memsahib...meri buchee ko bachalo...Memsahib take —
pushed like an unlooked-for gift into my arms.
She turned into the smoke and steam.
I never saw her face.

As we lumbered off I unwrapped
a dirty, days-old girl, too weak for cries.
Her bird weight and fever-filled eyes
already put her out of our reach. By Murree Junction
that child would have emptied half our beds.

At the next water-stop my nurses left her.
The corporal whose arms had gone looked up at me
and said, *There was nothing else to do.*
Gangrenous, he died at Murree a week later.
His eyes, I remember, were clear, deep and blue.

The Last Soldier

The last soldier marches out of the jungle
to the gentlemen of the press and an official welcome.
He salutes, presents the sword
which his parents, thirty years before,
had him swear to use with honour
in war, or on himself. Swathed
in a white cloth, it does not glint in the lights.
The President orders a reception, magnanimously
pardons the crimes of his private war.
A chartered Jumbo flies him home:
his mother's cheek is leather,
his father's mind has split.
The crowds scream for a walking-history,
the last spirit of Empire. Too late.
In his absence the Dream has come
and gone.

The bright shells of cars litter his path,
blind-eyed towers monster above him;
selling lights dazzle, pattern unfamiliar streets.
The air cloys with a sweet choking sin.

Back in the jungle, the fronds of evening
finger a clear sky, rainbow birds dash
colours across the deep green.
Minutely, against the background of birds
and the timed whispering of the ocean
his abandoned radio crackles into life:
orders come through.

The World

This is how it ends:

a finger slips —
two Russian subs resurrected
from the ocean
retaliate
before they drown.

California
the flat Mid-West
the Great Lakes cities
New York/Washington
— all clouds, acid air.
Europe's on fire.
The Third World eats
itself and starves.

In the far North
the Inuit
listen to their radios.
They move further North and
the North wind sweeps them clean.

This is how it ends

with the last family of Inuit
eating fallen caribou
pushing North
killing sick bears
going West.
Reaching the Bering Straits:
at the edge of the ice
a bloated seal at their feet.

And farther out floating
towards them on a floe
a man, a woman and child
waving spears.

From the Hills, the Town

As he talks he rolls an apple in his hands
which with the force of his thumbs
he splits to make two glistening
full-waxed moons of sweet flesh.
Below, the town is a mouth of broken teeth.
In his mind it is geometry, lines form a grid
— the runway, the mosques, the bread shops.
His face is a map of the long year.

Stones and mortars. But now it is a quiet time.
Though the day still has warmth, his men huddle
around a stove, the smoke of bacon, coffee.
He grows hungry, his eyes blink wide.
He fits the two apple halves back together
and bites from one, then the other.

The watchers

Brady's Glass

The senator's wife herself served us — tossed
fresh salad with the finest ham:
full cured Virginia, at god knows what cost,
the tomatoes somewhat underripe, but fat.

Our conversation turned to the war
— Lee's retreat and his scorching of the South —
until a crash of glass brought Silus
and the other boy to the door.

His barrow had tipped against the glasshouse, splinters
were scattered like ice all around. 'Brady's glass,'
the Senator said, 'his photographist's pictures
from Antietam, when we held against Jackson.

The dead at Sharpsburg, at the Bloody Lane —
most distressing. The public's sense of shock
was very regrettable. The plates he left
were just the size for hot house panes.'

Silus fitted fresh glass from a stock
he kept in the stables. Faint grey ghosts fallen
in a dirt road ditch with awkward limbs
and bloated bellies, backs arched in pain.

All that summer the sun shone through
those stiffened dead, printing them
on to the green leaves and ripening crop,
bruises in the fruit that were grey and blue.

The Captain's Diary

On the whole, a good year. By chance
the summer has left the grass full and strong
after our uncommonly late winter.
The new half of nine holes is settling down,
though the greens will, no doubt, need years longer.
Rabbits continue to create a damn nuisance;
the professional has borrowed a shotgun.

We have resolved at last, with common sense,
the issue of the women. Surely it is bad
enough encountering them on the course without ceding
government of the Tenby club to them. The ladies,
some of them, may play decently enough, but having
their own captain and secretary gives them
all the say they need without hampering
the business of the club with their chatter and whinge.
Now they have Miss Adela Voyle, if you please,
as their 'Captain' and the trappings of their own club.
All this won without platform, chains or a food syringe!

A greater number of visitors this summer.
Caught one fellow using a cleek — a cleek!
— off the seventh tee. 'Use a driver, sir!
A driver, if you please.' I sent him packing
and will keep an eye out for him in future.
These visitors contribute to the revenue lacking
but nothing justifies such impertinent cheek.

High tides will prove a problem should we persist
with those holes along the South Beach
for that fine prospect of Caldey Island and the coast.
The Rev. Morris proclaims that if God had
meant there to be a golf course here then He
would have marked one out. Sometimes Morris has a manner
too flip for the propriety of his calling.
 (I answered him with a belch.)
We were at the sherry decanter, be it said.
Though our most celebrated guest seemed to welcome
that sort of banter. His Majesty's Chancellor
proved to be a passable hitter of the ball,

though prone to take in the view too much
to consider seriously the challenge of the golfing.
It is said that he will cut a road
in the history of our empire. Certainly,
it is held to be a matter of note for the Welsh
that one of their number be counted in such office.

He is of no great height for a man of coming greatness
and his eyes dart at times like a goat's,
not wishing to miss one moment. Except on a tee,
I am here thinking of the Black Rock from which, as I say,
his gaze was something of a dreamer's.
'This land,' he said, (and all the time
to my intense irritation he called me 'Doctor M')
'it is as if a giant had scooped the grass and sand.
Or great engines of war had gouged the earth in bites,
that now grows back to heal its wounds.'
Which I thought smacked too fully of the poet
and too little of the real man.
Though, in truth, there were rifle cracklings aplenty
as we passed the Lifter's Cottage, playing the Railway
and holes through to the Penally Butts.

It is my belief that we have recovered completely,
as a body of sportsmen, if not in our fiscal health,
from the loss of that land to the Army.
What seemed indeed a hard blow four years ago when all
our efforts to build an 18-hole course were washed away
as surely as if the sea rose over us in storm,
we have now had to put behind us. The Army's needs etcetera...
Though Mr Lloyd George seemed not inclined to deal
with this German Navy business when the vicar,
that fool Morris, raised it at dinner.
For my part, I think the Powers shall resolve matters
as good managers ought with the world's affairs.
God preserve us from another engagement. The Boers...
These riflemen on the ranges at Penally are like
golfers at their practice. In readiness for the game.

The Tradesmen's Club issue has now been resolved.
I for one see little harm, provided their play
is restricted. They will prove useful in maintenance work.
However, the trial of the early closing day
free golf for the shop class could open up doors
best left closed. A course supervised by James Braid
Champion of the British Isles, must needs be strictly governed.
It was my honour to partner Braid in a medal fours.

Morris has word that Mathias-Thomas has bought the four holes
belonging to Davies's land. I think this bodes ill,
for while Lord Davies of Llandinam has much
to occupy himself with his empire of coals,
(not to mention Lloyd George's tilt at the Upper House)
Mathias-Thomas will surely look to catch a profit
from his acquisition. At the least my land —
the marshes up to Black Pool — is secure yet,
and could, if needed, bring some three further
holes into play. This land business,
and the continuing pressure for Sunday golf
darkens further the prospect of the impending winter.
Already the mornings are chill and the wind
from the Irish Sea cuts through tweed like a bayonet.

Home Front

That winter of our Island Fortress,
the docks blacked-out and sirens wailing,
the house closed its brittle silence around her.
Rain drummed the windows behind her children's dreams.
Over the months she saved from her widow's pay
and the hours of cleaning at the manse
seven silver coins, one from the abdication year
with the head of the love-lost king.

Should the coastline be split by incoming shells,
parachutes flower in the Vale
and jackboots strut in King's Square,
then she would lay her six children
to sleep, sealing the windows and doors
with newspapers and blankets.
Seven shillings' worth of gas
would deliver them out of occupation.

For months she has dreamt of his lost freighter,
torpedoed six days out of New York,
men overboard, gagging on salt and diesel.
How the ship reared and plunged like a whale,
her wash sweeping cold hands from flotsam.
As he sank into the anonymous dark
the final waves from her
minting coins from the constant moon.

Tonight the City of London burns
with St Paul's untouched at the very centre.
At the edge of night the Welsh ports sound no alarms.
She opens the curtains to a moon-bright sky,
counts out the coins in the tea-caddy
and holds them, cupped in her palms.
OMN. REX. Defender of the faith. Emperor of India.
The seven polished shillings sing in her hands.

Poles

An ancient woman in black
bends slowly over her row of beans.
The crop has come and gone and now
she pulls the yellow plants in bunches
out of the earth. She loosens
each pole of the row, then stretches to pull
the cross-stick which secures the length.
She works inch by inch,
a black shape against the shadows of the trees
and the whiteness of her ducks.
Passing down the road — Panzers, *Coca-Cola* trucks,
coaches of tourists. Beyond her plot
the sea in which we swim, from which we run
exhausted, tingling with salt, laughing.
Now she has raised the centre stick.
It balances on her finger tips like a javelin.
She lays it on the sheaf of spent poles
as they did at Thermopylae.

Dedicating the House of Art

For weeks we cleaned and dressed the town.
This was our festival, our moment.
A million hours of planning, sewing, embroidery.
We hammered nails into the night.

And all the important people came,
the trains were packed, there were
aeroplanes stitching the sky.

Our mayor and officials were lined in welcome.
This was a people saluting itself,
a new world of hope and possibility —
our Leader himself began as an artist,
a chicken farmer became chief of police.

The parade was hours long, following
the route of our great historical buildings
from the boulevard of the old Emperor
to the new House of Art.

Only the best were chosen —
the tallest with fair hair and features.
his was a Folk celebrating itself
as we wished to be. Knights on horseback,
foot soldiers with pikes and banners.
The tableaux of our women,
the warmth of our mothers, sisters and wives,
scenes of pastoral beauty in our land
pulled by oxen, great horses steaming in the sunshine.

Lifted on the shoulders of my father
I swayed to the music and the drum.
And our shouts, and our cheers.

The polished bronze of the sculptures,
the glistening paint of the canvases.
He proclaimed: We have cleansed
our art of the decadent, the modern,
the distortion of truth.

And each of those days, it seemed, was fine
without exception — blue skies, marshmallow clouds
Such times, such fortune,
we would nod to each other and say,
Hitler days.

Villanelle for a Photographer

0. Winston Link: *Hot Shot East at Iaeger. West Virginia, August 1956*

The smooching couple in the chrome saloon
Are teasing love in their fumbling way
As the Norfolk & Western steams before an August moon.

On the drive-in screen a wounded MIG plumes
Through a cold-war sky. Strategic blunders will betray
The smooching couple in the chrome saloon

Whose earnest gropings, sighs and moans
Counterpoint the loco's thrust and sway
As the Norfolk & Western steams before an August moon.

Link's wired-up lamps, set to jewel the gloom,
Flashlight the upholstered Fifties and display
The smooching couple in the chrome saloon.

What gung-ho promise drowns in a Korean monsoon
While marines act out some crude screenplay?
As the Norfolk & Western steams before an August moon,

Like train-crossed lovers in a soft-top tomb,
These clean-cut kids compose their dream in a Chevrolet,
The smooching couple in the chrome saloon
As the Norfolk & Western steams before an August moon.

Crane-flies

for Gareth

The foghorns keening in the bay
belie those sultry days.
September's Indian Summer:
our apple-tree's grown sweeter than ever,
hazelnuts ripen and brown,
there's a morning haze across the lawn.

This year so many crane-flies
— Daddy-long-legs —
each room in our house has a pair.
They whirr and tick, crucify
themselves in high corners, against lamps.

Yesterday you came from school hurt
that boys were pulling wings apart,
snapping flies' legs like twigs
until you threatened them with worse.
'Crane-flies,' you told me,
'the proper name is crane-flies.'
Your anger was wonderful,
I could have squeezed you till you cried

All the week the t.v. has brought us
the phalange massacres in Beirut —
mangled corpses parcelled in sheets.
'Goyim murders goyim, and they hang the Jew!'
Words, gunfire: the tangled lies of hate:
this will be called The September Slaughter.
It will blur into Middle East History.
I would not expect you to distinguish it
from all the other crimes even if you should
some day read it in a book.

Except, maybe the word 'September'
will set your hands fidgeting
and then you'll think of crane-flies,
drawn to our lights to die. Remember
how you caught them, held each one

beating in your cupped hands,
learning that sense of life
as a distant, other thing
that would fly if we gave it wing.

At Sligo, 1976

1

I was born in a town like this
— a river, a bridge, a road, a bay.
Market town drawing fish and the spoils
of the blistered land's hours.

Here in this rented bed
I hear the Saturday drunken shouts
cut through the day's travelling tiredness:
an hour's flight
from patchworked Wales,
sea blanketed with low cloud
before the sudden break into a Dublin morning,
the walls' graffiti

PROVOS KILL ALL BRITS

A slow train west across the flat land.

2.

Tonight after the official sherries,
in a side-street bar,
I & George and Marjorie from California
join the folk-night crowd
singing outoftune Johnny Cash
and other trash.
But all stand for The Soldier's Song
and, pissed, sway in a raucous patriotic mist.

In Carmarthen
the farm boys loud with money
after the Saturday mart
would swing at town men and students alike.
There is a facile purging
in the fists of drunks,
a hammering at the wall of life.

Here it's the flags that wrap enmity.
The drum and anthem
beat steady, sad time for the two Irelands.

3.

From Beesey Gallagher's Island
your eye reaches over Lough Gill to the border
past O'Rorke's Table, flat and round
as a drum.

Somewhere around thc curve of woods,
across that stretch of calm water,
the map's black line
warps men.

The Watchers

You are there
we can depend on you.
Speck on the screen,
white fly inching towards
the centre of the scanner.
And up above our warning station,
out over white clouds
over the grey fishing waters
your reality is a silver-glinting
massive hulk, four propellors flickering,
leisurely screwing.

A rear gunner waves
to the pilot of the Lightning:
a civilised greeting
in the blue whispering sky.

So factory worker, mid-shift,
housewife stretching shirts
up to the line,
miner scratching
in the guts of the land,
smile, you are appreciated.
The high silver Bear visits you
like a kind old uncle insisting
he immortalises the moment
in the eye of his box 'Brownie'.

The rattle of bullets in the trees

Lessons

Right up the edge of the pit
The Professor of History taught:

Every tree, every cry
Every tear, every leaf
Each death, each blade
Of grass. Remember everything!
We are scribes — one of us
Perhaps will survive
And be all our future.

The wet, black earth on our feet.
The rattle of bullets in the trees.
The sun jewelling that belt-buckle.

*

At Birkenau I saw one of your kind —
He was in the Sonderkommando at the crematoria
Scribbling lists by the light of the furnaces.
I snapped the pencil and tore the paper —
He said nothing.
We made him throw open the doors and put them in —

He was silent.
Then we shot him and fed him to the flames.
On my walk back to the barracks
I read his name in the sky.

Soup

One night our block leader set a competition:
two bowls of soup to the best teller of a tale.
That whole evening the hut filled with words —
tales from the old countries
of wolves and children
potions and love-sick herders
stupid woodsmen and crafty villagers.
Apple-blossom snowed from blue skies,
orphans discovered themselves royal.
Tales of greed and heroes and cunning survival,
soldiers of the Empires, the Church, the Reich.

And when they turned to me
I could not speak,
sunk in the horror of that place,
my throat a corridor of bones, my eyes
and nostrils clogged with self-pity.
'Speak,' they said, 'everyone has a story to tell.'
And so I closed my eyes and said:
I have no hunger for your bowls of soup, you see
I have just risen from the Shabbat meal —
my father has filled our glasses with wine,
bread has been broken, the maid has served fish.
Grandfather has sung, tears in his eyes, the old songs.
My mother holds her glass by the stem, lifts
it to her mouth, the red glow reflecting on her throat.
I go to her side and she kisses me for bed.
My grandfather's kiss is rough and soft like an apricot.
The sheets on my bed are crisp and flat
like the leaves of a book ...

I carried my prizes back to my bunk: one bowl
I hid, the other I stirred
and smelt a long time, so long
that it filled the cauldron of my head,
drowning a family of memories.

The Visit to Terezin

Here are the houses.
There is a light there, and listen
— someone sings.
How clean the streets, yes?
A tidy people, we have observed,
with their own pride.

Here is their bakery and, do you see,
a cobbler, carpenter, the butcher
with their own beliefs
in the killing for meat.
We come to the school. Later we will
be entertained by their orchestra.
A race is redeemed by music, I think.

Look at the children's pictures. You see —
houses with fences. The chimneys smoke
— there are families inside.
A giant — look at his club, his boots.
Where there are children, there will be giants.
And always butterflies, look, so many colours,
they use all the colours,
as large as kites, as large as clouds.
Where a child's mind flies, yes?
This one has played the gallows game.
Or it could be a door.

Trials

I believe nothing of this.
Nothing.

Lies infest these proceedings like lice
— a court of blind revenge.
You talk to me of gas chambers —
show me them. Photographs — faked.
A man in Dusseldorf wrote me —
Ah! You don't listen.

Hermine — she is my wife.
A loving wife since the time she came
to the United States of America.
She is a citizen these long years.
Like me — an American.
How should I believe these lies?
Revenge and emotion runs wild in there
— even in the public gallery a jew
dressed in the striped-pyjama camp things.

She worked in the office I tell you
— files, typing, numbers and lists.

So how could there be justice?

Ach — they say eight hundred and twenty
thousand pairs of shoes.
Jewelry, teeth, gold teeth,
a mountain of wedding rings. Where?
Show me these things — the proof.

Who kills children must be animals.
You believe that—
kicking them to death;
the Harvest Festival of open graves;
a german shepherd off the leash tearing
a pregnant woman apart —
all the stuff of propaganda,
horror stories of the Zionists.

Enough of this Maidanek. Let it rest.

American jews want these trials.
That Wiesenthal is a crazy man.
A hunter for thirty years — he
should learn to forget.
Let them all go to Phnom Penh, Uganda,
the Russians,
— let them put their scruples to the test.
All I know is that for me
it will be years more without her.
Can you understand the horror of that?

One night a blanket of snow
thick over the State of New York; the lines
down. I go with her in my dreams:
she moves ahead of me, turning
in the saddle, beckoning now
with her whip. She moves towards
the smoke rising in the trees, past
a straggling column of refugees.

Hermine, my wife, my woman,
my beautiful silver mare.

Portrait of the Painter Hans Theo Richter and his wife Gisela in Dresden, 1933

This is the perfect moment of love —
Her arm around his neck,
Holding a rose.

Her wisps of yellow hair
The light turns gold.
Her face is the moon to his earth.

Otto's studio wall glows
With the warm wheat glow
Of the loving couple.

This is after the dark etchings,
The blown faces. This is after Bapaume —
The sickly greens, the fallen browns.

She is a tree, her neck a swan's curved to him.
His hands enclose her left hand
Like folded wings.

This is before the fire-storm,
Before the black wind,
The city turned to broken teeth.

It is she who holds the rose to him,
Theo's eyes which lower in contentment
To the surgeon's smock he wears for painting.

This is the perfect moment,
The painted moment
She will not survive.
This is before the hair that flames,
The face that chars. This is before
Her long arms blacken like winter boughs.

This is the harvest of their love,
It is summer in the soul,
The moment they have made together.

From Otto's window the sounds of the day —
The baker's boy calling, a neighbour's wireless
Playing marches and then a speech.

Friedhof

They are tending the dead at Ypres.
The beech leaves, November bronze,
are lifted and rolled over
into rows between the slabs
by the gardener's blower
while three others follow to rake
the long mound and fork
this harvest into their barrows.

Behind the barbs of squared beech hedge
each yard of peace names its German dead,
twenty by twenty on dark, flat slabs
so that, without the steady sweepers,
you might come to this place as to a park,
tread the leaves in a path to the two figures
— a man, a woman; a father, a mother,
kneeling sharp and hunched before
some undetermined loss.

Years after the war, Kathe Kollwitz,
finding at last her only son's grave,
shaped these two from stone.
Now, his wooden cross a museum piece,
his name is flattened with the others
under this brief quilt of leaves.

At Tyn Cot, The New Irish Farm,
St Julien Dressing Station,
at Sanctuary Wood, at Lijssenthoek,
and a hundred cemeteries more,
the victorious dead, white-stoned, upright,
are ranked in the democracy of death —
Dorset, Welch, Highlander, Sikh,
Six men of the Chinese Labour Force.
The whole world bled through Flanders.

Turning the wet earth, Flemish farmers
still find wire and bones
tangled with the potatoes and beet.
And, occasionally, the local paper

carries at the bottom of a page —
Farmer blinded by shell.
It happens when they remove the detonator
from the rusty casing. The trade is well
established. The explosive is tired
but has a pedigree right enough for the men
of Armagh, Fermanagh, Crossmaglen.

Boxes

for Jenkin Williams

My train draws its way across England
through the stations of the harvest —
box-acres of grass rising lush and green
after this year's rainy June,
hay swathed into shapes that match the sea's
slow, summer waves in July.
And now, a half-cut field with lines,
geometric curves and parallels where tractor
or lovers have laid paths like ropes
to hold the swelling weight of summer.
The smooth wheat flanks of Gloucestershire and Wiltshire
and crops turned to stubble, with hay bales,
then, wonderfully, caught in one swirling field of rye
a masss of the brightest poppies.

Over distant London the 747s are strung like barrage balloons.
Now, Jenkin, I remember your story:
you flew as gunner/navigator in a Mitchell.
On such a morning in '43, six squadrons
rose from fields to the south and east
and formed over Southampton for France.
But one squadron of Dutch crews excitedly
broke radio silence and forced you all back.
So that afternoon you re-formed and once more
flew south to Cherbourg and the rocket sites.
The Germans, fore-warned, raised a box barrage
— shrapnel solid between six and eight thousand feet —
that scythed through the bombing formation.
You fused, aimed and dropped the load at speed, then
swung around, putting her nose to the coast.
A swarm of Messerschmitts tore the stragglers to pieces.
It was then your mid-gunner caught some flak —
shrapnel took half his jaw away
You left your maps to comfort him
and held his bloody head in your lap.
A rough ride all the way back
keeping low across the sea,
and you thinking *It's not me,*
Iseu Grist, poor sod, it's him, not me.

Three days later, a clear, warm Sunday in July,
you took the long, slow train back to Wales
and his parents' home in Tredegar.
Beside you on the seat, his belongings in a tied box.
Across Berkshire, Wiltshire, all the farm counties
were turning to stubble, with hay bales
and then, wonderfully caught in one swirling field of rye
a mass of the brightest poppies.

Kalavryta

Like a tattoo on the wrist — 13. 12. 43.
Those numerals underwrite everything.
This martyred town insists its destiny.

Under the square's ancient plane tree
The exasperated gauleiter fists in angry hectoring.
Like a tattoo on the wrist — 13. 12. 43.

All males over 15, step forward. Come with me!
Up the track to Kapes Hill, forced marching.
This martyred town insists its destiny.

His machine-gunners' calloused hands rake efficiently,
Their smoke and steam in the cold air engraving
Like a tattoo on the wrist —13. 12. 43.

They bled the snow into icons of misery.
The hall clock's hands stuck at 2.34., unmoving.
This martyred town insists its destiny.

Now pines confer their summer cones, falling free
Around the close crypt heady with candles' memories
                                                        flaming.
Like a tattoo on the wrist — 13. 12. 43.
This martyred town insists its destiny.

Greece

The Bowl and the Spoon

Behind the high wire
In a hut under the stilted towers
two women face each other.
Between them a wooden bowl and a spoon.

Each in turn takes the spoon.
They hold the bowl with care,
like a rare porcelain, firm,
concentrating the eyes, the fingers.

A spoonful, a spoonful,
another dry swallow,
so that still the bowl
holds its same level of soup.

After a while and without words
the daughter at her turn lifts
a spoonful away from her dry mouth
and puts it to her mother's.

She takes the soup, then with her turn
feeds her daughter. In this way
the bowl is tilted and emptied,
only in this way is the spoon licked dry.

A full moon has risen through the wire
like a cut cheese. Light
cat-licks the bowl and spoon
on the bare table.

In this world this is the love we make —
to the strongest the food,
the life to come. Our only grail an empty spoon.

This drawing of lines from memory

Sporting Frieze

For thirteen years that house wrapped itself snug
around me. The landscape of childhood:
the brass toasting-fork no-one ever used,
a vigilant lifeboatman, a chalk dog,
the cracks in the grate like map contours;
my dead, unknown grandfather framed, and the bellringers;
a huge box of cars and trucks and Meccano in the cwtch.
At night under the bedclothes with spies, Germans and Indians:

through all the Stalag tunnelings,
Tail-End Charlie night-raids over France,
our frontier cabin surrounded and ablaze, above me
the jolly pigs pranced and kicked and bowled,
sent stumps flying, bulged goal-nets.
An unbroken frieze that ran on past our moving
until Gran's late death. A month ago we rummaged junk
in that shrunk and cluttered back-room.

I wish I'd had the sense to cut and peel
a strip from the wall.
It all went under the decorator's knife,
with the faded lino, curtains and doors —
a short blaze of rubbish in the garden.
I should have brought the pigs back to this house,
hung them in a frame, behind glass in my room,
safe, and found like a poem.

Couples from the Fifties

Vague shapes stiff and grey all those miles away
The Coronation in our front-room — dull monotype, limited edition.

*

I smelt the Alvis's leather back seat as my father's radio declared
War on Egypt — the Suez route to India. East of Anthony Eden.

*

Mau Mau. Eoka, National Service. Singapore, Berlin. The war won,
the Empire dimming, the curtains coming down.

*

Rock 'n' Roll came to Carmarthen, two years late — the usherettes
Amazed as kids jived in the Lyric's aisles, just like the Pathé News

*

Buddy, Elvis, Cliff, Gene, the original Comets and Bill.
The sweetest love-song ya ever heard — Don and Phil.

*

The outcasts, the lunch-time loners, the misunderstood,
We trekked to the lost geyser springs of Fecci's espresso.

*

Coffee steam blends with Woodbine smoke and through it all
The Mekon juke-box doing slow-motion card tricks.

*

In Blackpool I held out my autograph book for David Nixon —
    in colour!
Who made cards machine-gun, vanish, then float back into view like
    gulls.

*

Dad's challenge — up the Lynton hill in the little black Austin,
    first gear:
then back down on the brake to what the sea had left of the sea-wall,
    Lynmouth.

*

In the grey-dark matinees of the Lyric I plundered
The idea of oysters in a coral reef of petticoats.

Pictures in a School Hall

Rows of old school photographs
Lined like tombstones along the wall
of the stifled, polished hall;
Firm, structural, they bear the weight
Of the years like slabs.
1st Rowing IV 1922 — oars held firm
By these men-boys in their sack-like shorts:
Sweat on the river, remember brothers, fathers
Dead. War-games past, normality is spooned
Out of the placid water. Images of bank and tree
Rise to the surface as the wake of the boat fades.
1st VI 1933 — prim girls in long, white knife-pleated
Skirts hold their racquets, alien as snow-shoes.
And the summer evenings bounced away
While, distantly, a civilization rocked
With the shouts of the crowd.
1st XV 1939 — arms folded over their chests,
Puffed like robins, hair cropped and oiled,
These boys look like our fathers.
And the master, young, upright,
His moustache and stance mark him
As an officer of cavalry come too late,
One of 'the few' perhaps.
And out of these games came a war, more wars,
A turning of the world back to stale beginnings.

The Grammar

They were never dull, those half-remembered,
half-composed men, our masters.

We joined with them in some conspiracy
(the grey-trousered 'Fifties needed authority)

and the hurts they did us dull down the years,
those classroom NCO's from some distant war of tears.

Some had survived, like Jenkins Chem whose face
was one big scar from when his tank bought it at Falaise.

Others missed the show, or dodged the chance to fight:
they lived through peacetime's sterile wank.

Perhaps they took it out on us, the celebration
fruit of victory over Hitler and the Japs; a generation

not long enough on the branch, fallen,
rotten on coffee and juke-box rock'n'roll.

We made them the stuff of boyhood myth, and all
colluded in that corridored game they played.

We had the hatred of all arty things
an all-male institution brings:

Roberts Music played us Chopin, the poof,
but set us shivering with that Mussorgsky stuff.

Ethy the Art taught nothing us at all. Smutty
Michaelangeloes, we'd draw in his David's classical balls

and rather die than meet him behind the board
— hands on flies, backs to the wall.

Maths when Bonzo Davies would chalk backwards on a dap
BONZO — and print it on your bum with a public wack.

And all the time the skirmishings ran on:
their job to keep us under the thumb;

our skill in changing words of the hymns
and silent, riotous farting in the assembly gyms.

Then stinging ears, arse canings.
A system of rude awakenings.

Those well-remembered, rarely-composed men, our masters,
coloured in our formative years, the clever bastards.

Great Uncle Charlie

1893-1980

What better way to end it all
than this January day,
the fields across to Peasmore fresh with rain
and Enbourne's church, St Michael
and All Angels held in seven centuries of air;
the grave's sides of polished Berkshire clay?

Now the month-old holly lies in our hearth,
spikes curled and brown,
but the berries' fire still glows
red as the poppy in his wreath.

The last time we saw him alive,
a week before Christmas,
was in the cottage hospital flanked
by two of the dying, the obviously dying,
his mouth slack and eyes closed,
until our voices woke him
and he smiled. His eyes brightened
and widened under the full, white head of hair.
He shook our hands, that odd
grip with two finger-ends lost
in the press at Simpson's the printers
where he'd been apprenticed as a lad.
Pronounced unfit with a dicky heart
for Haig's trenches, he'd lived
to see this century to its last gasp.

For an hour and a half he kept us talking,
flirting with a nurse, joking with the tea-lady.
Then I brought him round to the war:
They chose me from the ambulance men
and had me dressed in full uniform
to drive the old King to Reading,
to the station where they brought the wounded in.
Rows and rows of stretchers along the platform.
And a band playing full blast.
Old George, he stopped every yard or so,
and some of 'em (and here Charlie lowered his voice

in deference to those dying at his sides)
had no . . . (he touched his arm) *and some of 'em
no* (and here his leg). *An'you know
what his majesty said — he said, Don't
you worry my man (and most of 'em were
no more than boys) don't you worry he said,
we shall soon have you back and fighting the Hun.'*
Charlie's eyes focussed away to the far wall.
*One morning Mrs Cooper at Thatcham
lost all three of her sons.
Same morning.
On the Somme.*

Before driving back we took
armfuls of ripe holly from his tree
at the backdoor.
              *D'you know
how that tree came to be here?
One day I left my spade in the earth
and a robin perched there.*

That holly was no higher than myself
and just out of shot as we posed for family snaps
— Uncle and Dad and Mum and Gran and me
pulling at my slack bow and arrow.
My father's jacket bulging with coins,
keys, tobacco, just like Charlie's,
his hand gripping a pipe, the other
clenched in his pocket, just like Charlie's.

Great Uncle Charlie,
you survive all the characters.
I place you at the wheel of a Ford Pop,
chugging to the top of the Air-Balloon.
Perched on that hill like a climber
looking back towards Berkshire,
you're rubbing tobacco in your palm,
packing it down in the bowl as if those finger
-stumps had been fashioned for the act.

The match flares for a moment
and the smoke catches in a wind that
twists it up and over your face. From below
it seems, almost, a halo.

Pine Baron

The spiky swift gestures
of an avenue of pines
and under them, this still-life:

the helmet Karl Kuerner wore on the Marne,
a sniper decorated by the Crown Prince.
Here his wife Anna uses it as a scuttle

loaded with dry cones to start her fires.
It is part of their farm now,
like a bucket or a cooking pot.

But what brings my jeep
jamming to a halt
right by that helmet on its brown blanket of needles

are the pitchy ridges of the cones,
with the sheen of oiled feathers, the curve of ears.
— They burn like a dream — she says.

A painting by Andrew Wyeth

Lines at Barry

Morning light steely and sharp on the docks-water
and beyond, outlining a ship in the grey Channel.
At berth, one banana ship white against the old mill building
where, you say, a forest of masts grew in the sun,
filling your great-grandfather's vision
as he rounded Friar's Point.

Ten days rowing from Fishguard
the length of South Wales. 1898.
Your grandmother lived her first week
in that small boat as they hugged the shore,
sheltering each night where lights marked
fire and food and life.

This is not a unique story:
each dip of his creaking blades pulling
towards coal, English and the new century.

Twenty years on he was carpenter to the town,
settled and secure in his middle life.
They'd worked all night to build a platform
for the notables, under the Stars and Stripes,
the Red Dragon, the Union Jack.
The next day he took his place in the crowd
around King's Square and stretched for a view.
This is where the Yanks first came in,
eight days rolled across the ocean
then marched in columns up from the packed, grey harbour.
The doughboys formed in dress order,
spreading and flexing their sea-legs,
the men bound in puttees, their officers' boots glowing,
the strange, stiff-brimmed campaign hats,
lines of polished Springfields raised against the Kaiser.

And for a moment between the speeches,
the cheering, the singing and the drill,
for a moment the lines were still and erect
as those distant masts had been for a moment still,
when the only sound was the sound of the tide pulling
his tiny boat: he saw again Sarah's tired smile,

the baby pressed to her nipple and sucking,
sucking hard, as if nothing else, not even he,
existed.
As this new morning goes, the haze
lifts slowly from the Channel, unveils
the munitions ship with her red flags up
and lighters packed with shells
drawing lines of foam to the smack centre of her sides.

Three lifetimes, two wars running to this moment —
and none of this is unique, this telling,
this drawing from memory of lines
where, steely-silver, what we are now
touches everything that made us,
and is dangerous, and shines.

At Ochrid Lake

for Zoran Anchevski

After the monastery of Sveta Naum,
after the frescoes and the blank spaces
of the stolen frescoes,
after the poems and cameras
and the sound-crew man who played for us
James Taylor on his guitar, we swim
beneath the mountains
in the lake's shallow warmth,
feet curling over the smooth, muddy pebbles.

Around the headland Albania's
border-posts, visa checks. the guard's cold eyes.
Across the lake are the blue-distant Greek hills.
Macedonia wedged into the Balkans —
tyrannized, subjugated, partitioned
by Greeks, Serbs, Bulgars, Turks, Nazis,
the Austro-Hungarian Empire,
century after century.

Zoran, once you climbed in these mountains
to find still the scars of the Great War —
shallow trenches cut into the rocks,
brambles of wire, shells, skulls
bleached white like great birds' eggs.

Beneath the hills
from the shadowed groves at our backs
pure water springs from the ground,
gathers into a river that courses
a current clear through the lake.

As we wade from the shallows
further into the flow, the river hits
us like a wall of cold. Suddenly
icy the water's caress turns
to manacles locked around our legs —
it is like the promise of death, then
under this faultless sky,
like death itself.

Belgium: Coffee

Over the Channel England and France
are held in the same small cabin window
and what parts us seems barely chance,
a length of ship-creased water.

Coffee is served over France and Belgium
with the villages and ploughed fields
laid out neatly between the clouds
that catch and buffet the plane.

Here where it is flat and rich we turned
before the Blitzkrieg and fell back in disorder,
in ill-fitting uniforms, rifles kept from Ypres.
Horses were drowned, trucks ditched and burned.

The ragged flotilla — weekend fishing boats
pleasure-trippers, anything that would float,
ferried home those dregs of an army
that in time became mythologically cheery.

These clouds held dog-fights
on such summer days as this — the height
we have gives us a grand view
down over the blue air they smoked through.

As we descend, bumping through cumulus,
he illuminates the Fasten Seat Belt sign,
the drinks trolley clatters and coffee, mine,
spills hot and sticky on my leg.

Reg Webb

had sailed the five oceans
putting out from Cardiff, Singapore, Boston,
he'd cork-screwed merchantmen
through icy shoals of Atlantic U-boats, then
in peace, piloted the fat oil hulks through
the maze of the Haven's rocky green and blue,
with their confusion of pipes to nuzzle
and suckle the Milford terminals.

Reg, landlocked for years in an armchair
in front of the tv's babble, stared
at his chipboard fire-place, the china,
chintz and brass, the gaudy gilt mirror.
Awash with bile, incontinent, bilges leaking,
his eyes watery and vast, was past pottering
with the roses and bulbs of the flat's
flower border, and shooing away cats.

Reg, becalmed in the straits of morphine
captaining his bed, full-sheeted, trim,
away from the port of his front room and tv,
the photo at the Palace for his O.B.E.
floundering and sick of being ill
sank angrily, far out in the cottage hospital.
He's lost now, with fire in the hold, and a hard stoke
for one last evasive action, making smoke.

Guard Duty

A cold spring morning in Berlin.
On the Grotewohl-Strasse the rising light reveals
no ghosts — cleaning women in head scarves flirt
with the passing soldiers. From his tower
the guard views the banalities of life in the East.
This vigilance too is banal, routine,
now no-one risks the wire, the sprint
across the seeded ground.

April 30th 1945.
Forty years on that earth-mound between the lines
is all that remains of the place.
The Unteroffizier loosens the top button of his uniform
and fingers the warmth of his throat; he imagines
that man, sallow, death-grey, his features soft as putty,
how at last he saw clearly the end of it all.
His fall was in the manner of such men of destiny:
Bonaparte wasting away the years on Elba,
pacing in a room wallpapered with arsenic roses;
months before the news escaped they'd shot the Tsar,
the Romanov family, servants, even their spaniel —
all went under the waters of an abandoned quarry;
and this last, closer defeat — *il Duce*
and his whore gunned down at Lake Como
then left to dance from streetlamps
a week in the Piazzale Loreto.

In the bunker he shot first his dogs; they'd whined
and bristled for days as the Russian thunder rolled from the East.
Then Eva, draining poison in the last act of her opera.
Finally, the pistol went to his head,
his nostrils catching the reek of petrol
from the cans lined along the corridor.
Like some stuffed effigy king and queen they were dragged
into the Chancellery garden, stacked on the hurried pyre.
Just a little, Aryan smoke wrote a coda to *Mein Kampf*.

Halfway through his watch, bored on this day
as any other, the guard lifts his gun
to follow a crow landing on the earth-mound.

It scissors its untidy wings and pecks away
at a worm. He snugs the Kalashnikov into his shoulder,
drawing the sights in line
with its bobbing head. He purses
his lips like a boy at play
knowing he could squeeze the trigger,
startle the thing into so many bloody pieces.

Veteran: South Dakota 1978

If you were in demolition
taking out the bridges
as the marines fell back.
If you were ordered to cut down
the women and kids,
leave everything dead.
If you swung round like
the workings of a clock
and scythed the three officers instead,
fragged them good —
if all that's true, then I'm with you.

But if saying this is your trick,
your way of living
with the fact you'd really
killed those peasants
(given the war and the VC
and not knowing
one gook from another
and it's making a better story that way)
then this party is flaking off
from your head like used skin
and I'm far from home
and reason and the neat confusions
that make poetry.

Manoeuvres on Kinder Scout

Reaching Kinder's river-bed
after a morning's trek
and the game is on.
Sheep silhouetted against the grey sky
become Apache look-outs
the boys dodge. They
follow the twisting river,
keeping low to the sandy bottom
as it drains the Kinder plateau,
running to spill at the Downfall's sheer drop.
We head South with the water
oozing between high peat walls
that block all landscape,
all escape under the blanket sky.
The boys run small risks,
soakings as they leap boulders
over the gathering force of the water.
Arrow-noises zing and zip
from their mouths into the spongy banks.

I let them whoop ahead and occupy
myself in walking. Then,
turning a bend, come across them
in a hushed huddle. The eldest boy, Routledge,
cups a ball of fluff in his hands.
Feet away, a hen grouse waddles back
and forth for our attention —
'I'm bigger, take me, I'm bigger.'
A nursery-book sacrifice.
Routledge smiles, makes a fist to hold
her chick, helpless, brushed with beginnings
of colour. Then, like some pageant hero,
he lowers that blind ball of feathers
to the heather roots.

He turns and leads us on.
One asks, 'Why...?'
'There's some things you didn't oughta...'
Hen and chick melt back into the scrub
before our boot-marks can fill
and fade in water.

We unpack lunch
sitting on the edge of the world.
At Kinder Downfall the peat-trickles bunch
into a tumbling rush of water
the windy uplift turns to mist
that bathes us. Light spumes off the plovers
that catch and ride the air's power.
The talking dies — we are breathless at the show.

All morning, we've crossed the plateau,
so, watered and fed now, we turn for home.
Mission complete, the schoolboy platoon
races on beyond my ken to Grindsbrook Clough.
Climbing the parapet of one more peat-gulley
I find myself alone,
the wind scouring my ears like shells,
my eyes loaded by the span of humped peat.
The world is weighed under loss.
Now, pinned to this map's one contour,
I see, stark and simple, the reality
of an absolute:
         this levelled
table-top world spread above its two poles
— Manchester, Sheffield —
and those cities laid waste
in a terror of nuclear heat,
brick and flesh charred peat-black
in a sear of thick light.

         Strange snows
will cover this mountain.
That history is held sure,
deep in the darkness of the peat,
deep below the jagged hulk
of a Dornier, its pilot's fist
clenched for thirty years.
That bomber, overshooting factories,
the web of searchlights, slides down
year by year to its real target.

Window seat to Chicago

Low cloud
banked over the western Atlantic
like arctic snow
puffed and ridged so
that if a bear should blunder
across it on all fours
I'd smile down,
watch it move on its belly,
fur-flop over the edge into icy water.

Imagine the fur swept back swim-sleek
and the paws stretching and heaving through,
its snout conning the surface
and the eyes narrowed, the claws sprung
by an ache in the belly.

A whale's shadow cuts the horizon
before the whaler's prow
mushrooms out its harpoon
and crashes the dream.

In McDonough County

for Fred and Nancy Jones

Waiting for you this morning
alone and chilled in the empty house
I walked out, crossing the road and ditch to the fields.
Miles of corn, October brown rising
firm out of the black earth.

As far as the sky it stretched
and what I had taken for a block of colour, a mass
of uniform growth, showed itself particular, alive —
the electric whine of crickets, their clicked-finger jumps,
a fox, a racoon, crashing through the lines.
The corn moves in the prairie breeze,
stalks and drooping leaves that scratch
and tap against each other — the whole landscape
like the flaking skin and bristles of this world.

The sky was wider than the eye could hold —
blue with a light hand of cloud below
the high streaks of jet planes.
I felt into the hanging pods
to the smooth, full barrels of maize.

Now, at uneasy midnight, I am woken
by a low, wide rumbling — lights spark
and turn out there in the blackness.
They are working through the night
to beat the threat of rain — combines
chewing down the rows, ruling the farms' geometry.
In the damp morning light their chutes
will pour rich fountains, gold atoms
splashing into the trucks.

Dakota, Nebraska, Illinois, Iowa, Ohio —
across this vast Mid-West
the grain silos rise like cased Havanas
blunt, silver missiles.
On a high-nineties August day, without warning,
you say, one explodes.

Land Army Photographs

How lumpy and warlike you all looked,
leaning against the back of a truck,
hair permed underneath headscarves;
in make-up, corduroys, with long woollen socks
— the uniform completed by a khaki shirt and tie.

You are posed in a harvest field:
long wooden rakes and open necks in one
of those hot wartime summers. Fifteen of you
squinting into the camera,
and the weaselly Welsh farmer, arms folded,
his cap set at an angle
that would be jaunty for anyone else.
He's sitting there in the middle, not really
knowing about Hitler, or wanting to know,
but glad to have all those girls
with their English accents and their laughs.

Mother, how young you look, hair back, dungarees,
a man's head at your shoulder.
You girls cleared scrub-land, burned gorse,
eyes weeping as the smoke blew back;
milked cows and watched pigs slaughtered.
You, who could not drive,
drove tractors with spiked metal wheels, trucks.
And once, on the Tenby to Pembroke road,
along the Ridgeway, they had you working flax.
For two days only it bloomed,
the most delicate blue flowers.
Like wading into a field of water.

I see you piling the gorse. Dried spikes
flaring into silver ferns, and smoke
twisting from the piles as the wind comes in
gusts, cool from the sea, the gulls drifting
lazily on the flow.

            And then,
one of them, too steady, too level, becoming
a Sunderland coasting in to Milford Haven:

over Skomer, Skokholm, Rat Island, over the deep water;
and, though you do not know it, over a man
who is smoking, scraping field potatoes
for the searchlight crew's supper,
who pulls and unpeels the rabbit they have trapped,
joints and throws it into the steaming stew,
the oil-drum perched over an open fire;
the man who looks up, the man who is my father,
watching the white belly of that flying boat
cut into the Haven.